Tales
of the
Mind

To order additional copies of this book, contact:
Xlibris
844-714-8691
www.Xlibris.com
Orders@Xlibris.com

ISBN:	Softcover	978-1-4500-7200-7
	Hardcover	978-1-4500-7201-4
	EBook	978-1-6698-1110-7

Library of Congress Control Number: 2010904428

Print information available on the last page.

Rev. date: 02/10/2022

Dragonfly

The dragonfly, nothing but a demon in disguise. They might seem harmless from our world. But on the other side, they're something more. We may not see it in time, but they always try to stay out of sight. The dragonfly is nothing but a demon's ride. Where the dragon goes, the demons go. And where the demons go, trouble starts to happen unnoticeably slow. But no need to fear because that slow trouble will soon turn to a pool of demon tears. Because if they're spotted out of place, they have nowhere to escape. How this works depends on how much faith we have in the Lord. This means we really play a critical role in this process. Don't mind this creature because faith depends and starts with all of us.

BREAKFAST IN THE CITY

In the middle of everet street, to the bays by the sea,

There's a town I once knew called Tiffany City. here by the beach is where I lie, enjoying the ocean's breeze, as I watch the wind blow into the jet stream,

I notice a wave coming from the sea.

I watch how it moves and moves and how it twists.

I was so focused that I couldn't resist, feeling in the air.

I notice music everywhere;

I notice a hidden sound that I once heard out of town, from where the sound had awakened me, to the shop that I had been sleeping. waking up in the streets, to me, was just another day in tiffany city.

East coast of saturn's rings

In our solar system's depths in space,

Saturn's ring's lie firmly in place.

They tend to tip a certain direction,

On the east coast way beyond Saturn's perception.

The rings are pointing at something scientists don't see,

A form of dark matter that will affect the lives of you and me.

The question is, what could it be?

It's too far away from the visions of the telescopes we bring;

The only clue is that they point at two directions,

Above and below Saturn's position.

Could this be heaven and hell?

No one knows; it's too complicated to tell.

It's fact that the rings will one day be gone,

Meaning the two entities had collided into one.

No one knows what to believe,

So I ask you this final question, what do you think?

Dear Dream Weaver in the Skies of Time

Dear Dream weaver in the skies of time,
I wish you to weave a dream of mine.
Please don't think badly of me;
I just want to dream in peace.
I want a dream of paradise,
A kind of dream that you would like,
For I would dream in the pit of time,

A dream reaching to your place of paradise.
I beg you; please, think kindly of me;
For God is your real identity.
Please put peace into my family,
Then bless my home with peace and symphony.
I sincerely thank you, God,
For you will forever be in my heart.

Eyes in the Skies

The time we visually see behind, are presence of the stars in the sky. But before our now-modern time, there was a sacred being that died. Nonbelievers thought he was gone forever, but the real believers knew he would always be there. Sometimes when we look up in the sky, we picture of many faces up high. But these pictures paint a small figment of a much bigger face in the sky, a face of the purist soul who died to save our lives. Some say he didn't exist; some discard him because they don't know what he is. But this pure soul gave us many gifts, which makes a characteristic in us somewhat unique and different from others. This is the man on the cross, who is known by the name of Jesus.

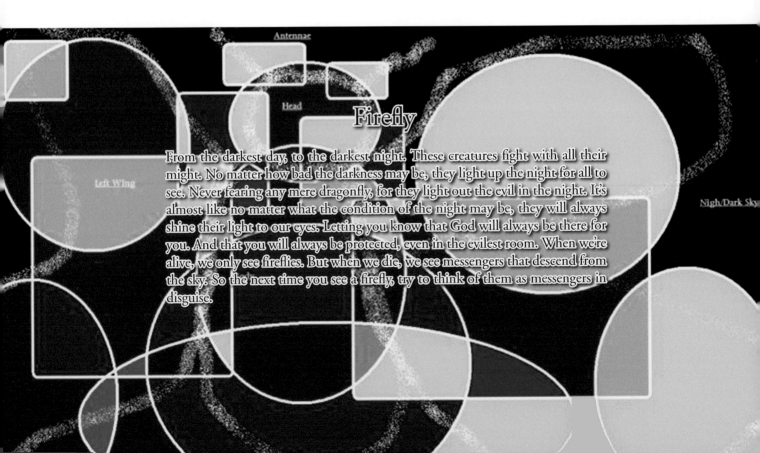

Antennae

Head

Left Wing

Nigh/Dark Sky

Firefly

From the darkest day, to the darkest night. These creatures fight with all their might. No matter how bad the darkness may be, they light up the night for all to see. Never fearing any mere dragonfly, for they light out the evil in the night. It's almost like no matter what the condition of the night may be, they will always shine their light to our eyes. Letting you know that God will always be there for you. And that you will always be protected, even in the evilest room. When we're alive, we only see fireflies. But when we die, we see messengers that descend from the sky. So the next time you see a firefly, try to think of them as messengers in disguise.

Hallway of heaven

From the abyss of arrows, to the knights of storming farrows, to the whistling wind of change, to the days we will be saved, going through the cosmos of life, heading into the natures of holy light, hidden within this light, there lies a door, leading to a brick path never seen before, as the path leads into the history of time, passing the palace of heaven's light, then the path splits into two directions—one direction is a path that leads to the lives that are never mentioned; the other is a stairway growing within, giving you the direction to the hallway of heaven. getting there is your mission, for god knows what you make with your decisions. within the hallway of heaven are books of the sins you have made. to be forgiven, you must repent to god and pray, for when the judgment road comes, it is the last day you see for when everyone is gone. god bless us.

In the Eyes of a Child

These lives of you and me come from one we all speak. Between the depths of space is where our worlds come face-to-face. This is where he delivers his gifts, far away and safe from the dark abyss. As the gift departs from its creator, it will take nine months for it to reach us in the new world. Then the day comes for it to open its eyes, as this gift carries a soul of life. A new star is born, until it leaves us. That day is when we mourn its name. Even if it has passed away, its love for us still stays. This gift is misunderstood by us, but the day it saves us is the day we are spared for its love and compassion for us. We still celebrate him today. He gave us the eyes of a child, which most of us can only hold on for a while. What a child sees is what we can't see. A sixth sense of perception, which sees the Lord's eye of what might happen. The demons we can't see are what children sense very quickly. It's not their imagination of what they see; it's the demons that are still breathing. It's not their fault they are scared of the darkness that surrounds them; we just don't see what's really frightening them. Ever heard something call your name, but you see nothing there? That's the guardian that protects you, and the one who fights for you. Although you can't see it. It's the gift given by the eyes of a child. The child who tears light. Who gave you this sight.

Lights

As a source, it carries a powerful force. If in the hands of the Lord, it creates life and so much more. Despite of today's present darkness, the light will always shine through this madness. Forever and ever, to the day we cease to exist in the universe. Amen to these people; amen to the life we're given. Amen to Christ, and amen to God.

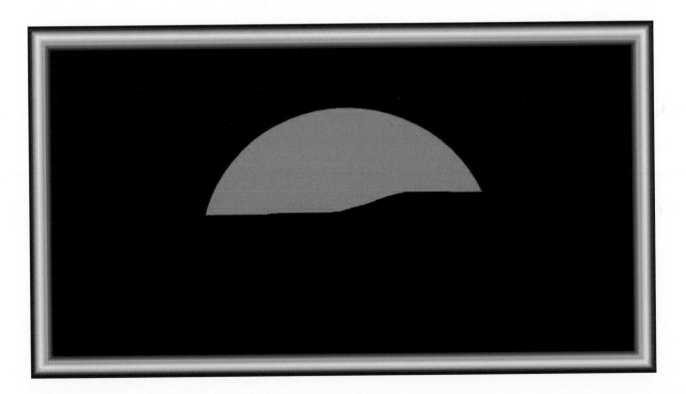

LOVE FOR THE LOST

As sad as it seems, there are lives whose faith seems to be depleting. From this cause, there are demons that tear their love apart. These lives are considered the lost, souls that need to be introduced to God's love. We can help them, but it depends on them to change. For the fact that they might go their own way. If they don't seem to go agree with the Lord, then pray for them so they can move forward. So if you're one of those who just help others, and you don't know why. The answer values your heart at a priceless cost; it's because you have love for the lost.

Mountains of the Messengers

At the highest landmarks lie the mountains of the messengers. But not where you would usually think it might be; it's where your soul speaks. The characteristics relate to feelings every day, a usual symbol of love or when it breaks. It's a main source to a singer's ballad that gives that soul the power to make us dance. It's a crushing feeling of losing a loved one; it's the faith given to everyone. A common symbol of the higher power, to depths of one's highest tower. It can make us do miracles out of the blue; it can make us calm tides to red moon. It's a source that keeps us believing, a source that stops at nothing to help the needy. Like a lightning storm, it hits you hard. Because it's all nothing but the power of your heart. That's the highest landmark; it's your loving heart.

MY DARK SIDE OF THE MOON

The moon we always see;
You see the bright side of me.
From a cause of good luck,
We seem to always look up.
But there's a side we don't see,
Known as the dark side of me,
The side that's bathed in sunlight,
For I can walk in the light,
But the side that is bathed in maroon,

Is my dark side of the moon.
From black to maroon
Is my internal moon.
I can take it higher,
Without suffering from my fire,
But as far as you can see,
You can't walk on that side of me.
From the opposites of my universe,
This dark side of me will always be my adversity.

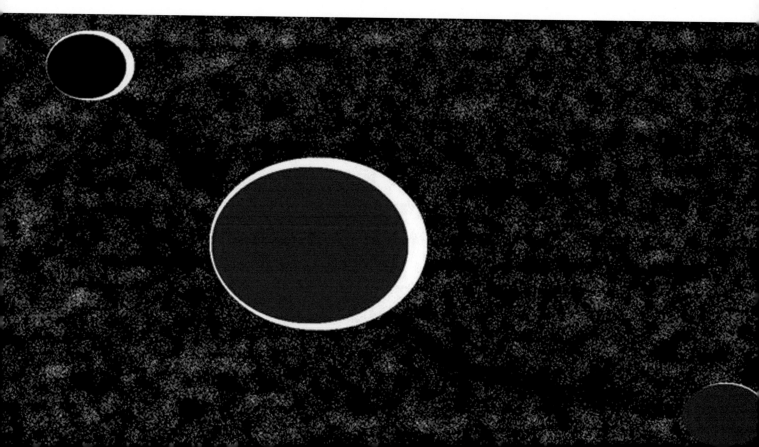

NIGHTS

There's a time in a day where sins are committed in so many ways. These are nights that show almost everything a formidable fright. As many things happen in the night, the sins almost shroud any sign of life. But think twice because the night is part of our beloved paradise.

The Kingdom from Above

From the heavens up high, there's a kingdom in the sky. From he who created all, to the beauty of the falls. As time goes by, we seem closer to the sky. As the misty morning rises, our souls come back from the horizon. As morning turns into day, children come out to play. As day turns into night, our souls go out for a midnight flight. As days go by, our father watches us high up in the skies. There are many reasons why, but some don't care, for they're blind. Don't tempt them, and let them be. For someday, our Lord shall let them see. Because every day is another day he lets us see, and we should be thankful and pray for holy peace. For Lord is my shepherd, and Jesus is my savior. For we unite together; we face our fears and dangers. If we are strong at heart and believe in the Lord, there will be no more. Arguments will occur every now and then, but that does not mean to start a war again. For a war already exists. Between the good and the evil, and that the good protect our people. As humans we have sinned a lot, but we're God's children. Our goal is to his heart. When we die, we have to go through Jesus. For he is the son of God, and he believes in us. It's never too late to start all over again, if you believe in him. He will forever fill your heart within; God bless you. Amen.

SEPARATE WAYS

It started on a rainy Saturday night; the clouds were gray and blue, almost as dark as maroon, as expansive as my mind is. some things you believe are just too furtive. hidden in the night lies a terrible torrent that kills me inside. as they all say love hurts, I don't believe there's anything to ameliorate how I feel deep within me. I once thought that she made me rapt, but instead she possesses my broken heart in her hands. just as lightning shatters the windows afar, it's her shattering my heart, as the retaliating feelings appear. I'm so stricken with fear, as I was so preoccupied to what might happen. here I am being capitulated to nothing, as she ascends that mountain. here I am pondering in the middle of the county, as my depression deteriorates. I find nothing immaculate; as arduous as I was to think, she was innocuous, till she made my feelings deplete. from the hollow darkness inside of me, there lies a formidable monster waiting to be freed. as the shattered dreams in my eyes turn to evilness inside this red light, as I'm trying to escape, this evil madness pulls my soul away, for I am one who lost faith in the lord. my decisions led me to fiery doors. as she took my heart away from me. so I took her life away so the beast can be freed. don't follow how I threw my life away; save yourself and believe what the lord has to say, for I've died sinfully young. my soul is now burnt and hung. be free and move on, for I am now long gone. waiting at hell's gates, so shall I wait for the savior to take my soul away.

The Bullet of Deception

From the dark grounds that I walk
Lie grotesque beasts that stalk,
Creatures drenched in blood,
Cowards to the holy one above,
Carrying and shooting arms,
Leaving their bullet mark on our beloved bonds,
Lying, cheating to themselves and others,
Showing no forgiveness, upon them and each other,
Restless and sick to their hearts,
Not realizing what they're doing to the world,
Maniacally vulnerable to their own creations,
Not knowing which way leads the right direction,
Becoming sinners of their own kind,
Giving no light in the darkness to find,
Confusing the wrong with the right,
Giving them nothing worth to fight.
The things they give us in perception are nothing but the bullet of deception.

The COSMOS of Life

The *cosmos* of life is a place out in space; the universe we seek is a beauty of work of the holy one we meet. From where the seven days God created earth, there lies an answer to a mystery waiting to be discovered, this mystery is somewhat similar to the question of life; the answer is our hearts, not in our minds. The visual you can't see is only visible to those who see with their hearts, a different kind of mystery that God has left for us to discover, and the discoverer is . . . *you*!

The Criminal and the Homeless Man

Once long ago, there lived two men down at Key Largo. They were best friends, but each had the same problem. They were both poor, and each man had their own idea in solving this situation. One man decided to help others with yard work and cleaning the roads. This slow process gave him little money, but it helped him survive out in the world. The other man decided to be a criminal—lying, deceiving, and hurting others to make his own dirty money. This process brought much faster profit than his homeless friend's currency did. Then one rainy day, the criminal bought a home in the suburbs. He showed his still-homeless friend the house and told him how he made the money by being a criminal forever. When he offered his friend to live in the house, his friend politely rejected and told his friend that he would rather be in the streets and would rather be well respected. The criminal laughed in a humorous manner, then patted his friend on the shoulder. Five days later, the criminal purchased a car. He offered the car to his friend, but the homeless man refused to accept any part of a car. The criminal could not believe what he was seeing, so he grabbed the keys and sped down the street. The next day, the criminal offered the homeless man a job. When his friend didn't accept, the criminal beat him down and called him a slob. After the attack, he left the homeless man on the street, sobbing. When the next morning came, the criminal's life was done. Left out lifeless in an alley, suffered his last moments in agony. But for the homeless man, the city recognized him as a model citizen. Helping giving millions of dollars to charity, and praying for his old friend to be in the hands of God's safety. Who would've thought a homeless man could succeed in little amounts, and have his wife and kids inherit over five billion dollars in his name? The last thing he wrote in his will was to build a statue of his old friend in the middle of town. To celebrate the day they became friends, and to celebrate their last days on planet Earth. Amen.

The Freebird

The freebird is a creature of heaven,
A known enemy of the dark raven,
A bird of many things
That connects the bond between you and me.
As we know, this bird's life was once an egg,
When the egg hatched, a new life became.
Unlike other birds,
This bird had no predators.
From the day it hatched, to the days it matured,
This bird blew through every obstacle as if nevermore,
With such great achievements,
Started with such great missions,
Missions such as faith, love, loyalty, respect, and kindness
That reward the freebird to live in this wilderness.
We should take this bird and use it as a role model
So when we get stuck, we have something to follow.

The only thing you should know about this poem is that who is the freebird?

The Freed and the Unforgiven

From the depths in space, there lies a solar system firmly in place. Within this solar system lies planets orbiting a star; in one of these planets lie life forms whose destinies stretch out far. Neither of their destinies are the same, nor are their destinies different. But it's these destinies that they reach out for each other, whether for freedom or for their own reasons. Their decisions either make themselves the freed or the unforgiven. Whatever the future may hold for them, it all depends on their decisions. To be the freed, you need to do the right thing. Because the place for the unforgiven is not heaven.

The Midnight Blues of Tomorrow

From the breeching heavens to the seas of earth,
There's a whistling howl passing by our universe.
Funny how the night moves,
Travelling as the sound of old-tuned blues,
Singing in the nether lands of sorrow,
Known as the midnight blues of tomorrow,
Saying, "Take me to the magic of the moment,
On a glorious night, to the end of tomorrow."
Then it gives us dreams,
Of the lives of you and me.

As it goes through our minds,
We leave our pasts behind,
To the winds of time,
To where the holy one hails high.
Now it's gone from our time,
Bringing our sun the horizon to shine its light,
Heading to our father's abyss of arrows
Go the tuneful midnight blues of tomorrow.

By David Nathaniel Rodriguez

The Midnight Dance

The midnight dance is a special time on Christmas Day, a time when the angels come out to celebrate. You might question, "Celebrate what?" It's to celebrate the day Jesus came to us. Nobody can say that that's not a reason for the universe to celebrate this special day. Because it's one of the few times we meet a descendant from God. This is why everything is so jolly and why you always feel music in the air that day. We're not the only ones that celebrate because there's always a bright new star born on that day. In fact, the star that gave direction to Jesus's coming still shines today on behalf of his loving. Santa Claus, elves, reindeer, and other tales of today are just displays of the emotion coming on Christmas Day. So when it's that day, you know whom to pray.

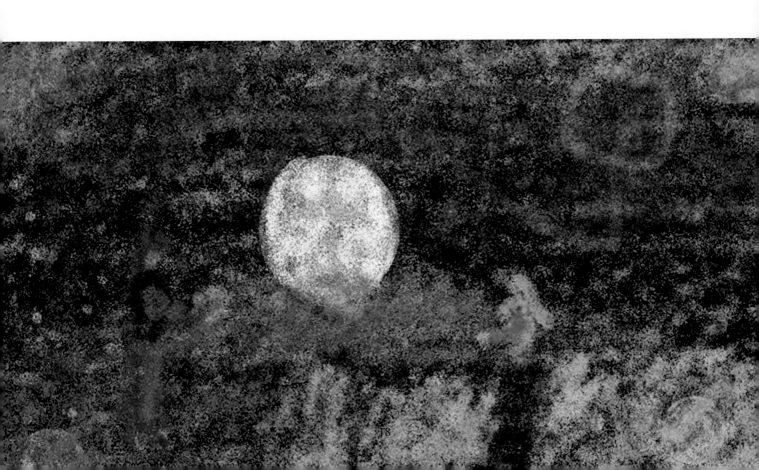

The Rainmaker

In these dark clouds lies a spirit that washes away our cares and problems. This spirit can also give life, but only to those who follow the light. He is not God, or a decepter of our bonds. He's just a special messenger, like the Piano Man, Wind of Change, Firefly, and Dreamweaver. He is responsible for the showers in the sky, as he watches us up high. The showers that he brings are his tears of joy and peace. As his tears fall down his face, they wash our worries away. When time passes, a moment of peace is brought upon the villages. Love is restored in our hearts during that one moment, then everything is back to its original state. Of course, love is broken when one has passed away, then tears of sorrow fall from his place. Every emotion and every feeling are raindrops that fall to your feet. Tears of sorrow, tears of pain. These tears keep the world safe. It rains when there's negative energy in the air, letting you know that God will always be there. This is as far as he goes now to wish you a loving farewell.

The Rose

The rose is an immaculate symbol of a deep feeling. A feeling of love, soberness, intuition, and even death. These are some feelings the rose represents. Though it's unwieldy that it represents creation, there plays another factor in this role, also now known as the end of the universe. But how is this possible? We recognize the rose as an innocuous flower that represents the beautiful feeling of emotion. More as a beginning of all relationships, not a destroyer of worlds. The real answer is simple. The rose has a shape-shifting meaning. In other words, the rose is not always red. The black rose represents the ending of a life's time. The white rose represents a demure angel from the heavens, giving the life of a newborn child a soul. Pink roses are accidently mistaken to compensate someone, or to celebrate Valentine's Day. The real meaning, however, is to give an epitome of how you really feel about that person. The yellow rose represents an explicit source of life. Almost like the sun. A green rose gives an example of a young life maturing into an adult. Now, the red rose has a mixed representation of the elements of life. Primarily the representation of the expansive universe. Creating and abashing itself as it expands. It can represent diminishing lives. Or, as the purple rose represents, retaliation! A sense of huge anger. Not to utter the blue rose's meaning. Though the blue rose actually means the torrent of love. Also the breaking of love. This rose has a powerful meaning. A similar rose, but sky blue, represents having a mainstay of wisdom. As you see, these are not banal representations. You can have a full lifetime odyssey by just studying what these representations mean. If you receive a rose from someone, look at its color. Try to figure out its meaning. That person might be saying you're like a kiss from a rose on the gray. Try pondering on what they mean. So the next time you're outside, pan around the area for roses. One of them just might be waiting for you, as long as there are many moods.

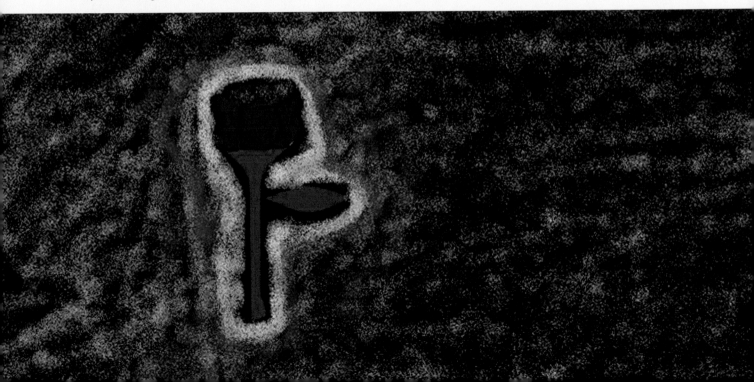

The Rose of Emotion

Thou shall not be confused with fact and emotion. Nor be confused with beauty and greater good. Take this rose as an example of beauty and emotion. And your main worry as a fact. Compare and find a similar bond between the rose and the worry. Once you have successfully found the bond, that worry will be nothing but a story. And that story will pass on as the greater good in you.

The shooting star

Oh, the shooting star,
As far as we know they are,
As they fall through night and day,
They break the earth for holy fate.
We're not different from thee,
Although some stars could never see,
In the cosmos we are all,
Although some stars will fall.
When we burn out, we drift through space.
For those who are damned will forever lose holy faith.
As our father leads us, we go through dimensions;
For those who don't follow up will forever never be mentioned.

As we dance into the night,
We fly with all our might.
If we fly away from home,
We'll forever be alone,
And if we politely stay,
Will wait for our father's holy grace.
This is our life through stars,
But to the holy, we're brothers in bonds,
As we wander through loneliness.
We follow the light to our father's heavenly home.
Good night.

THE STRONG-HEARTED ANGEL

No one may be perfect as the son of God, but many can be strong willed at heart. It's not from what it comes at logical explanations, but from the heart filled with temptations. One thing logic can never explain or define is what's being given from your heart and mind. Nor can it explain the things that people sacrifice to do the right thing. Just because you're not the most perfect person in the world doesn't mean you're not a strong-hearted angel-in-disguise to the Lord.

WIND OF CHANGE

The wind of change have you ever wondered what wind is like, ever had a thought or a wonder of mind, ever noticed that the wind felt different from before, from a steady state to a gust storm. Maybe it is us who make it different, or a dancing rhythm going with the wind; maybe it is something more, not a storm, maybe something that is long passed from before. Can it feel, can it move, or is it a door to another world, a sound of pouring sorrow, or the howl of the storm in the hollows, for we won't know what it will be, but to me, it's a creation of god's beauty. Ever heard of the wind of change. Does that saying flow freely through your veins, as the midnight blues go through the abyss of arrows? The wind of change comes to the seasons of tomorrow; unlike the midnight blues of tomorrow, this wind goes through your soul, destroying your sorrow, but what could it be, just ask god for he has asked me. As it goes through our windows, I feel it flowing freely through my pillow, if you're at a loved one's funeral, you feel it when thinking about the times you spent together; that's the wind of change. You know this because a wind gust comes, passing through the plain. The wind of change is not something you see; it's what you feel, as it passes through the trees. As it passes into the pit of time, we feel only what it has left behind. From the dreamweaver's flute, to the seas of earth, from the shooting star to heaven's door porch, it takes any shape or form, into a prophet that had once lived before. We know this man very well, as he rose from his grave. Saying he will always be here in our hearts, it is he who lives in our dreams and it is he we think about when we rise to the next day. All we have to do is listen closely; you hear that? That's the wind of change.

Animals and Spirits

From the land we roam, we find creatures that show we're not alone. What we also find in the world are lost spirits finding their way in these unknown parts. Animals and spirits continuously interact and bump into each other when that happens. We humans wonder what is going on around them. For animals, for some reason they sense things we can't sense, feel things we can't feel. Hear things we can't hear and see things we can't see. Yet another example of having a keen sixth sense of perception. It's no wonder nothing doesn't capture their attention. Then what about spirits? What do they have to do with this? As far as we humans know, there are two types of spirits. Ones that deceive us and ones that try to show our father's blessings. When animals sense their presence, they would most likely act in ways we can't imagine. For the spirits, they either move on or don't forgive. The reason I bring this to the attention is that we must not fear either of them. No matter how scary or weird they seem, we must not forget that the Lord's heart is the place to be. For that he loves and protects us. We'll always be safe, even after we see Jesus.

The Guitar and the Piano Man

David Nathaniel Rodriguez

Once in a town living in the suburbs, there lived a man who would play his piano. He would play it until the sun set southern. Then one afternoon, he saw a guitar sitting by the window. A guitar that had once belonged to a widow. He picked it up, try some notes. But he just couldn't get the right notes. He wanted to learn how to play the guitar, but he didn't know where or when to start. On the fall of midnight, to where day breaks into night. He prayed to the skies of time, prayed that night, that one day, he would play his guitar to his paradise's time. Then he felt tired, and went to bed. For God was awake, setting a plan ahead. First he decided to put the man in a trance, then he set the dreamweaver to the man's bed. By then, the man was asleep, an effect that came from God's keep. When the dreamweaver had left, he had left a sparkle inside the man's head. By morning, he had woke from his unsupressed snoring. The man still didn't know how to play the guitar, but didn't stop him. Because he had something inside him that was reaching towards heart. But this thing inside him brung the rhythm if sway. Then on the eight day of playing at heart, the man's work finally brought out the sound of a harp. From there, a sound of a guitar playing rhythm strings in the air. As he continued further, he cried to God "Father please take me further!", then from the thrust of his arms. He whipped out a music of nature to a song from his guitar. As the sweat drenches the clothes he has worn, this man kept going until he would outlive this storm. When everything passed, he noticed that the light went to the corner, then he realized that daytime was almost over. When he looked at his piano, the piano that brought him famous all the way to his last gig in Seattle. When the noises had stopped dead, all he could think about were the ideas in his head. "What next?" he said.

Printed in the United States
by Baker & Taylor Publisher Services